vast
self *poems by*
KV Wilt

POINTER OAK

Pointer Oak / Tri S Foundation
Distributed by Millichap Books
millichapbooks.com
shamanzone.com

These poems first appeared the following publications:
Red Rock Review
    "Split in Half by Shadows"
Cantilever
    "I Believe," "In the Beginning," "Apparition on Abbey Street,"
    "The Buses of Feda O'Donnail"
Crosscurrents
    "Eurydice Is," "I Was Too Young a Lover,"
    "Orpheus Sweating," "Orpheus Builds the Fire"
Creative Loafing
    "Red Isis," which won the Red Contest for poetry
Sandhill Review
    "Saint Leo Waterworks," "Lost on the Longestdarkestday,"
    "The Glass Scarab"
Gulf Stream Review
    "Moth"
Third Wednesday
    "The Dream Is Like Real Life"
Throwing Stones
    "Vermeer's Woman Weighing Gold: for Denise,"
    "Stuck With Snack Duty: Camp Lenape, 1963,"
    "My Beautiful: for Mabel Ramsburg Wilt,"
    "Louise the Medicine Lady: Lajes AFB, Azores, 1950"
Poetry Salzburg Review
    "In Clonbara," "Orpheus in Ballaghderg"
Bicycle Review
    "When the Makos Came"

First edition. First printing
ISBN 978-1-937462-26-0

We ourselves are the Vast Self, that One Actor in the universe who creates continually in all moments. We are the Vast Self playing in creation as creatures, as individuals. In the experiences of my life, through loss and transformation, ceremony, and story, I learned how to emerge continually from the individual self that is Joseph Earl Head Rael into the Vast Self again. In the kiva, in sweat lodge, in the sun and long dances, I have learned to die to myself in order to know the Self, dying from this House of Shattering Light into states of ecstasy, and then returning again, that the Vast Self might drink continually the light that It is creating.

JOSEPH RAEL
House of Shattering Light 199

DEDICATION

These are among the favorite poems I've written. I dedicate this collection to Denise and Yasmine who have beautified my life.

I also dedicate it to Joseph Rael, the Pueblo/Ute shaman and storyteller whose friendship has graced us. May he live long and continue to benefit all our relations.

Several of these poems incorporate Tiwa/Pueblo words, and most incorporate Pueblo principles and sensitivities.

Finally, I honor Dave Oliphant and David Craig who have guided my writing and Francis Rico, Lanie Anderson, Paulette Millichap, Carl Brune, and Pat Crerand who bettered this collection.

Tutah ('love,' 'center,' 'kiva' in Tiwa)

Contents

VAST SELF

Vast Self
(*WA-CHI-WHO* IN TIWA)

In each granule—
galaxies; in each air
sac—atmosphere; in each flare—
stars; in each bottomless hole—

black beginning. In
each unforged, feral word—
Blake; each predatory song bird—
Whitman; each shape shifting

incantation—Orpheus. As
each twice born Taliesen
who tricks beaver mind
to smash its dam, who scares

away the bats that nest
in the skull's soft spot,
who charm cobra
from its basket—

Vastness.

Nah

(TIWA FOR 'SOUL')

Nah
is the pit house
in the chest
where sun and moon
love on buffalo robes
and bear skins
where sage smolders
on the altar
where mountain lion curls
around the emergence hole
on the juniper roof
where red ants
architects of the Anasazi
coin red clay
where stone walls bend
to the beat of wings
the slap of fins
and the thump of drums.

Beautiful Painted Arrow
BERNALILLO, 1983

From his backyard sweat lodge,
Painted Arrow's light body
was pulled above *Posu-gai-hoo-oo,*
'Where Water Slides Down the Arroyo,'
into a crown of crimson
elders. Why hadn't their shaman
built the vibrating chamber
they'd shown him in visions. Before
he could say he hadn't found a
pristine place for the first kiva,
the fiery wheel of archangels
spun him back into the middle
of his garden. The incandescent
ancient ones were the resonant
walls around him. The axis,
the *sibapu* of first emergence.

Yggdrasil

Yggdrasil is
spotted eagles
at the top of the ash
bringing and stitching twigs
is
pencil-nosed moles
underneath
doodling on the root roof
is
the horned borer beetle
curled in the trunk's core
rocking on its wing case
is
the leopard slug
on the longest limb
painting a night-glow line,
touching up the horizon
with its tentacles.

Dancing at Zuni
(A:SHIWI)

The 100-degree sun sets. Behind his back. Behind
Twin Buttes.
He's on the adobe roof above the dirt-packed
dance plaza.
Looking down. Leaning on the only ladder. Whose
rails taper
through clouds. Four clown kachinas, in the East,
forty feet
across the plaza, wear helmet masks collared with
black fur and
juniper. Reminding him of sea urchins and
Christmas wreaths.
The clowns seek something on four sides. Probing
loose stones,
open windows, a woman's skirt, even a sleeping
dog, with their
sticks. Prayer sticks, says the young kachina carver
beside him.
The clowns find five or six mudheads in the South.
The mudheads, smeared with grey clay, wear no
shirts or shoes.
Just little skirts and kerchiefs. And a bulbous bag
mask that
looks like a potato sprouting eyes. Nightmare.
Some have
rattles and feathers. Macaw or magpie. The
clowns prod the
mudheads' private parts. Tribal members, stacked
on three levels
of roofs, laugh. More mudheads salt the square.

From the North.
From Holy Corn Mountain. Play leap frog,
yelp like prairie dogs,
roll like armadillos. He hangs over the roof.
The kachina carver
grabs his belt. The clowns lasso the
mudheads into a dusky cloud.
And funnel the cloud through the window,
over the corn altar in
the West.

How Magpie Became a Koshare
('HOLY CLOWN,' 'TRICKSTER')

Every night Magpie pretends
to fall asleep till his wife rends
the veil, rises from their bed
and wends to the Pleiades,
where she descends seven steps.
Magpie follows her steps' echo
until he reaches the top
of the kiva where he stops.

In the black hole, holy clowns
lead Corn Woman across rainbows
but fall. "A robber's on the roof,"
they say. "Bring him in the womb."
They drop the would-be shaman
onto the lap of Corn Woman.
Where his braided cranium bursts
spraying the crypt with fireworks.

The Glass Scarab

FOR FRANCIS RICO

The glass scarab
from the antique store
in Alexandria
was supposed to be onyx.

The canary colored
iris leaping through jasmine
toward the fire engine door
was supposed to be an orchid.

The gold-green-red-blue-white
polyester prayer flags
Lama Lha brought from Lhasa
were supposed to be silk.

The lanky grey beard
tending glowing stones
with crow's feet and wings
was supposed to be a man.

The Bard at the Eleusis Bar
WINTER SOLSTICE

Is the bard slouched
in the doorway
chanting odd bars
in an arcane tongue,
strumming filaments
our eyes can't see?

Do his shut eyes
and Cheshire grin
signal he scored a pint
or is his unleashed soul
skipping rungs
on the ladder to Elysium?

Is the glowing butt
between his fingers
Persephone's torch?
The filthy black bird
filching his frozen bread
the messenger of death?

Poets play possum.
Don't near the portal
or the trickster will seize
your leg, steal your heart,
and yank your seed
from its perishable cone

on the shortest, coldest,
darkest day of the year.

Shamans and Muse

FOR PAULETTE MILLICHAP

Hooting from
its iron roost
on the rusty water tower

barred owl spooks
the spindly-legged hound
thirteen stories below

shadowing
the string of storefronts
facing town square.

A swamp rat
from no-man's land
behind the fire station

tiptoes through
the dim intersection
toward the trash can

teaming with
unfinished fast food
outside the post office

but veers off
when it hears the hound
paw the cracked pavement

then pee on
the metal hooves
of the mailbox.

Sprinting toward
the square, the rat
skirts the white oak where

three shamans
spotted by a streetlight
lean over a black Mercedes

fine tuning
its platinum engine
with ivory fingers

polishing
its glistening back
with deerskin gloves

dropping tears
that hit its onyx hood
and turn to pearls

that slither
off its epaulettes
on dirt and dry oak leaves.

In the east
a cheap bulb clicks
on behind the mist.

From its den
deep in the Earth
the north wind stirs,

belly crawls
toward the south
along clammy ground,

uncovers
the ankles of night things
forgotten in the fog.

Dressed in black
cotton to her calves
the milk-white muse

walks barefoot
through the wet grass
strung with the harps of spiders,

steps elk-like
over concrete crumbled
by the August sun.

Surefooted
she climbs star by star
through constellations,

wades into
the icy rapids
of the Milky Way,

veils herself
with the sheer lace
of dying nebulae.

The mail truck
from Athens downshifts
in the intersection.

Celestial Eyes

The young girl
leaves her parents
praying at the shrine.

She paces to
the lotus pond where
goldfish crease the surface

of a blue cloud.
The murmur of her
parents' prayer is muted

by warbling wrens.
She sits on the rim,
removes her sandals,

slips one calf
then the next through
the opal cloud, stirring

the bowl like soup,
brushing its bottom
with her weasel hair feet.

The cloud moves
over the temple. Sighing,
she sees the sun's rays dive

to the bottom
where she feels, then sees
celestial eyes nibble her toes.

For Emily Dickinson

MADWOMAN

When she wrote "Madness is Divinest Sense,"
she meant the thread connecting most heads
to sublime is sometimes a rope from which
a mad poet hangs, feet fixed in heaven,
watching humankind's cruel habituations.
Minerva's blue bird described the labyrinth
the right-side-up tread, the depth of the trench,
the hubris with which the strong trample
the weak, and the shadowy escape doors
the faithful ignore. To them the bluebird
who preferred the forest to the walls,
the valley to the track, and the chanson
to the oath was a dangerous failure.

Split in Half by Shadows
RILKE THE MINK

Propped against the door frame
with his long slim fingers
slipped into his pockets
and his upper body
split in half by shadow,
Rainer Maria
peers over his moustache
like a curious mink.
Under the influence
of the moon, the mink
creeps halfway out its den,
Duino Castle,
to expose its silk coat
to the constellations.

Unseen, it scans the silver-
plated fields for images
it digests in its den
to which it must return
before daylight or die.
All day long it dreams
of Childhood, of winged Things,
of myriad angels.
And in the end, instead
of becoming a gryphon
which grapples this world
and the next, the mink feels
wings sprout from its shoulders
and its paws disappear.

The Singer's Temple

I.

Upon his birth, Rilke
received a piano
to accompany the gift
of voice from Apollo.
The ragas he hummed
when young were a sign
that he had re-entered
the assembly line of time—
to bewitch hungry ghosts
and spark the weak-boned
to make a dance of woe.
His kestrel cry echoed
the ardor to defy
the fortress of the sky.

II.

Gaea's piano stood
in the house's marrow
while the unrooted poet
somersaulted in its shadow.
Till, intuiting his split,
Rilke offered Orpheus,
his muse, fifty-five sonnets
in praise of heaviness.
His instrument in dust,
he sang them 'in chapel,'
lamenting none of us
"has built the Singer's Temple."
The poet, by chanting down,
bound empyrean to ground.

ORPHEUS &
EURYDICE

I Am Not the Orpheus

of sunscreen and crowded beaches,
bustling bars, and calling cards;
of whipped cream and luxury cars,
microwaves, multi-level marketing,
cell phones, bouquets, and billboards;
of zoos, high-heeled shoes, membership dues,
theme parks, paychecks, and tycoons.

I am the Orpheus seen
by the person in the back row,
the cross-legged Orpheus
wearing scuffed boots and overalls,
whose vertebrae fit the ridges
of an elephantine oak,
who chews sage leaves and watches rocks,
volcanic iron, suck the glow.

I am the Orpheus heard
by the barred owl in the oak
screening the moon, Orpheus
who transports stones in deer antlers
into the hole in the hut
shut out from outer light and scents,
who rubs sage on scarlet rocks,
his wet chest and forehead. Who prays.

Red Isis

FOR DENISE

Beloved, you've revealed
yourself in reds. I reel
in your ripe exuberance
that ambushes my senses.

When I was becoming
a young man, burgundy
pursued me everywhere
till I wore that wine sweater

all winter like an ensign.
At my middle age you're sun,
next door's rooster, mars, fox,
sweat lodge fires, four o'clocks,

and an Irish linen shirt woven
from cinnabar and vermillion.

I Was Too Young a Lover

I was too young a lover.
Orpheus was entertaining
friends. I followed the beekeeper
for his sweetness. The gathering
didn't see me leave. Orpheus
spellbound them with hymns and wine.
He still worshipped Dionysus,
deity of hive and vine.
What was the secret of his song?
Fire and water bound by fear?
Though Eros' power was strong,
I was the daughter of wind and air,
the sister of crane and curlew.
Faced with engulfing flames, I flew.

Since You Came, Eurydice

Since you came I shun
the harsh Aegean sun.
Athena I abandon
to her perch upon
the parched Parthenon.
I seek the conundrum
of convoluted rooms,
of caves and canyons
where your intuition
muzzles my deduction.
In this fifth season
when vision is clear,
you reappear.

Eurydice Is

Eurydice is your left hand,
the ebb tide's cursive in the sand;
the trembling that you won't disguise,
the unveiled longing in your eyes.

She is the ringing in your ears,
the transpiration of your tears;
the hall when violins stop,
the swallowed wine, its empty cup.

She is the melody you find
yourself singing, the twilight mind
that recollects dawn and foresees
the eyes of owls in the trees,

that hears their silent scimitar
rise and fall between the stars;
taproots burrowing towards the nave,
pale green seedlings breaching the grave.

Eurydice is the incense
in the nostrils before rain;
the smooth stones underneath the falls,
the rainbow trout hid in its pall.

She is the wail of the canyon,
the murmur of the mountain;
the afflatus of the sleeping
baby between waxing and waning.

Orpheus Builds the Fire

Cutting cedar into four-foot logs,
he envisions his spike-driving father
who came to Quebec City from the bogs
of Donegal. He lays the thigh-thick cedar
east to west over the raked coals
that form the platform of the pyramid.
His father, Fergus, was forty years old
when they stole his frozen body, hid it
from his Ojibway wife, and got their priest.
He takes the nineteen cold stones from the soul
of the lodge to the logs and invites the sacred
powers as he puts seven in a wheel.
He stacks the other twelve up to a peak.

In his voice he hears his father speak.

Orpheus Sweating

He sits in the absolute black
of the lodge, the new moon, the tomb.
He sits with the east to his back,
his face to stones in the womb,
each an orange sun glowing, singeing
his knees. He sighs a year's burden,
drops sage on the stones, starts singing
an eagle song his mother sang when
the sun rose. Sage rises to his nose
and eyes. He asks for clarity.
Then sings for deer, bear, and buffalo,
beseeching compassion, strength, peace.
From the lodge he crawls a little boy
soaked, dirty, weak, quaking with joy.

Old Orpheus

I.

I am an off-beat old man
    without a plan.
I am captivated by the words
    of mockingbirds,
waterfalls, wildflowers, hot stones,
    and sun-baked bones.
I pay attention to the muses,
    to the phases
of the moon, and the stations
    of the sun.
I am awed by those who don't know
    how much they glow
and dismayed by the ignorance
    that spurns difference.

II.

I've forsaken the mask;
    my prayers ask
for earth, water, fire, and wind
    to strip worn skin.
I see my elongated hands
    in the badlands,
undulated, sinewy, striated.
    When it's too late
to sleep, the goddess reads them.
    Her stare extends
through the screen, glass, and curtains
    relieving the pain
of not having a love
    up to my trove.

After Eurydice

That morning he arose
and couldn't recognize
the face of the old timer
staring from the silver
plate. Night had divorced
observer from observed.

Orpheus felt as if
he were a meteor, adrift
from senses and thought.
He took a piece of chalk
to capture the strange face
on a slab of slate.

As he mapped out the chin,
the image turned protean,
becoming alternately
stretching desert, vast sky,
deep lake, and broad meadow
where he spied a thing brown.

And he followed mole
into its narrow hole,
trusting his hands and feet
curling in its nest of peat.
He drew strength from iron
and didn't miss the sun.

Then he dived with beaver
into frigid water,
propelled by his broad tail,
holding his breath until
he reached the fort of sticks
and clawed into a niche.

When fish eagle rose
from liquid explosion,
a bass in its talons,
he leapt in the vacuum
of its Herculean flapping,
his arms becoming wings.

Sidewinder's diamonds
shimmied on the sand.
In the zigzagging fumes
his fore and rear limbs fused.
His belly, glowing coals,
swiveled through its hollow.

Thus he became a bard,
his love liberated
from one lover, one face,
one habitat, one race.

The Old Song

I want to sing the old song, the timeless song
of the cawing crow, the clapping thunderbird,
the squealing pig, the rushing waterfall, the bristling birch.
The song once sung by shrieking gypsies, howling dervishes,
whooping Sioux, wailing Bedouin, crooning trouvere.

My grandmother from County Cork hummed
some bars while washing dishes.
My grandfather from Genoa, who pretended to be wizard,
whistled a few bars when he dodged raindrops in his fedora.
Had they known they would have been ashamed,
so focused were they on forgetting,
so drunk on the Peabody, the Black Bottom, the Charleston,
the heady perfumes of the melting pot.

Today, people are the only silent species.
Their once-moist skulls are dry,
no longer watered by their hearts;
the seeds of perception shrivel in the field.
The old song has evaporated, turned back,
leaving the people bitter, like sucked straws,
mocha and mezcal flowing through their breasts.

If I could sing the old song,
stretching back through Jacob's ladder,
maybe the out-of-work Slav metal worker
in the next booth, awaiting a callback, pining
for a wife and child, would hear and involuntarily
thump his heel, bob his chin, bat his eye.
For a second his breath would sink,
his electrons jump their orbits,
and his ghost dance back into his body.

KIN / KEN

When the Makos Came

A cramp yanks up the log of your left half-leg with its horse-shoe-sized staples from the bleached sheets lying like executed sails. The nurse bales eggs to the fortress' portal, but your lips won't eat. The Jamaican nurse grunts as she straightens the yoke of your noble shoulders in the bed, only to sigh like ebb tide when you lean back to the right, wedging your monumental head against the cold aluminum bars that prevent you from dragging your gangrene home. Oh, Colossus of Rhodes, I was ten quivering years when we drove past the dome of the lunar-like satellite tracking station to our fishing spot and saw the gray whale, a washed-up continent, with stringy Bermudians trying to push it, lift it, pull its scimitar tail. When the makos came, the gray clenched its jelly jaws, listed its barnacled hull, and quivered its flukes in agony. I plunged under your stone-soft chest.

My Father's Earth and Fire

FOR YASMINE AND HL

Watering sage and roses,
we hear a tyrannosaurus
tractor traumatize the air.
Outwardly, I cringe;
inwardly I breathe down
to wake the stegosaurus.
Eight year-old Yasmine lashes
my waist with her white arms,
nestles her nose in my ribs
while her leashed rabbit darts
under the shrimp plants.

When I was her age,
a fishing boy in Bermuda,
I was our father's sidekick.
My hollow stomach shuddering,
I scaled his bellowing black dragon,
the Triumph, tightened my twigs
halfway around his trunk baring
the engine from my emptiness
as he rent ten-foot coral walls
enroute to the airbase woodshop
to manhandle the machines.

As he shaped the cedar logs
we'd cut from dead trees
the week before, I stood behind
in the swirling scent and sawdust,
fighting the high-pitched metal terror
that ripped, chiseled, chipped, sanded.
Anticipating the flicking of the switch,
the slowing down and stopping,
the passing down of bowls, lamps,
and candlesticks for me to polish.

The Death Lee Wished
ALAKUNUK, AK

By the time your
eyes began to blur,
your feet and hands
numbed, your toes
rotted, your bypass
could neither push
nor pull fluids,
and your fume-filled
bellows couldn't
extract oxygen,
you had already
denned in the CD's,
assumed a tunic
of sheet music
and dreamed
of being back
in Alakunuk
riding ice
into white.

The Dream is Like Real Life

FOR HL

I arrive with two Burger King coffees with cream.
The nursing home halls are deserted
save for the sentinel inside the door,
the nurses in their nests,
and Millie's faint scream for Mary.
I hear the History Channel
on the other side
of the white curtain.
I wake you.
You break back into the world
of amputation with a bang
like an oxygen starved diver
blurting "Kurt, is that you, SON?
Get me out of this bed!"
I cry inside my eyes.
No one has ever been so happy
to see me.
I drop the side rail from the bed
and maneuver the wheel chair
from the claustrophobic corner.
I lock the wheels
and slip a couple Dutch Masters
into the knitted pouch
underneath the seat
above the plastic urine bag
hung udderlike
between the wheels.

When I turn to take
you under the armpits

and pull you in the chair
to soon become a throne
you're not a man
scarred, carved, and blind
but a boy, a baby
limber, lively, and limbed
reaching with all fours
to be picked up.

Nursing Home
EZKEIEL'S WHEELS

Stationed at the portal's sides
like library lions, legless sentinels
soak smoke and sun, having navigated
down and out from the world of wheels.
They will scare you, but when greeted
these guardians will smile and talk small.
A Haitian patient usually rolled
our blind dad beside them. An angel
born and bred in Jamaica lighted
his cigar and listened to him tell
the places his doppelganger piloted
our Uncle Art dying down the hall.
The foyer is newly decorated,
camouflaged in flowers and pastels.
This check point is inhabited
by staff and administrative personnel.
Its wide, hollow wings are slated
for those who feed and wipe themselves.

Enter the elevator that ferries you
from the minor to major mysteries.
On the second floor, you'll smell fumes
of diapers, sweat, flesh, and memory—
of our parents, who, piece by piece, lose
every aptness humans beings envy.
Sue, down the hall from Dad, used to mew
"Mary, help me" day and night; and Mary,
beside Grandma, shouted, "I gotta do-do."
If you can bear the veneer of misery,
you can sense eternity seep through

the fear of the forgotten. While gravity
craves their hollow bones to infuse
the garden, their steel chariots, which carry
them from waiting room to waiting room,
also become four *hayyot*, heavenly
four-winged beings, who let them spoon
with their suitor, Death, until they marry.

The Light Might Jump

FOR JASON

when manymany normalbonemarrowcells
becomeabnormal
one doesn'tdiefrom brokenbones
one usuallydiesfrom toomuchfluid inthelungs
or toomuchurea or creatinine intheblood or
clotsinthebrain from irregularerratic heartbeating or

the lightmightjump fromthelamp.

Yellow Butterfly
FOR JEAN/ERIC

delighted by the lineaments
of dawn, you alighted in this place
of time and space where sleepers mistake
glamour for grace, certificates for sense.

too soon, the bones that beauty wed
succumbed. numb, we huddle in the night
while you flutter upward in the light.
winged sister, bless us who dwell in dread.

Eric Remembers Moonlight Bay

on that side
of the empty
jack-knifed bed
the picture windows
and palms promise
a pool.

so too the water-
color sunset hung
over the slack-
backed pastel chaise
on this side.

but not the grey-
maned man
sitting in it, half-
wrapped by a hospital
gown.

between the whale
jaw in front
and the half-sunken
ribs in Moonlight
Bay behind
the house

he bobs his question
mark,
rubs his bowling ball
knees
as if they were
crystal.

Eric and Glenn
FOR GT WILT

It was one
of those adventures:
the night before you two
left, you lashed your army-issue
ponchos across Dad's airplane inner tube
so you'd have somewhere to stash the conches
(whose innards you'd give to Mr. Price, your Bahamian
head cook, for chowder) and all the other treasure you'd
discover off Fort Desoto, but when you got out there, down
there, the conches had absconded and you were found nearly
out of air by that Mercedes-sized manta ray (for whom you
two-leggeds were treasure) who towed you toward Turks-
Caicos till your lungs said 'uncle' and you rose like
snowflakes, both of you, within a wet-suit arm's
length of that clanging buoy you clung to
shivering till sunup when the shrimpers
who sang "Stairway Way to Heaven"
again and again took you back to
Tarpon Springs, Andrea,
and Jean.

I Believe

FOR LOUISE CLARICE

I believe in four seasons,
in the holiness of trees,
the descent of leaves,
the resurrection of sap,
and the transpiration of vapor.
I believe in photosynthesis,
in the communion of chloroplasts,
in absorption of light,
the illumination of chlorophyll,
and the fluorescence of photons.
I believe in the Calvin cycle,
the incorporation of carbon
and the genesis of sugar.
I believe in the transformation of water
and the begetting of oxygen.
I believe in evergreen.

Louise the Medicine Lady
LAJES AFB, AZORES, 1950

Wolf, the base's German shepherd, led me to Terceira beach
to greet the fishermen coming from indigo with sardines. Which
I stuffed into my pockets. To Francisco Bigote of the nose and
moustache, who took us to the dank cantina. Where only men
could go. To the pool table which was a soccer field. To
Francisco's shoulders where I saw the balls crash, bounce, and
drop into black holes. Holes where Dad would drop his lines.
Where marlin, sharks and sword-fish swallowed you whole.

When I finished my limonada, Wolf led me to our house under
our landlady, the Portuguese widow who wore black. Whose
indentured servant, Alda, came down to teach us Portuguese,
to bake bread in the cavernous oven, to tuck us in. Whom Mom
bought from servitude and tried to adopt.

Mom, whom Azoreans called "Medicine Lady." Who sewed
Antonio's split tongue. Who saved Francisco's charcoaled toes
with salve and gauze. Who charmed Alda's migraine with
aspirin. Who splinted Serafina's thumb. Who told Mark and I
about Jonah and the whale. Who said prayers where we
disappeared.

The First Kurt Spoke

portuguese with a long
island accent. #2 chucked
cottage cheese on the living
room ceiling when his dad left
for greenland. #3 hit home
runs, bullied younger scouts, killed
little finned miracles and hooked
them to bait bigger ones. #4 cheated
at golf and vocabulary, pretending to be
#5, who sang rock & roll, drove a cab,
and took the morning-after pill. #6 wrote
heady poems with a penlight at night, for
eurydice, on a canvas bunk, slung in the bladder
of a wwII destroyer. #7 swigged baudelaire
and breton and published under the influence.
#8 flunked husbanding, friending and fathering.
#9 dug holes. #10 was pardoned by goddesses
and trees. #11 taught knotting and unknotting
to untouchables. #12 wished he had been born
with moccasins. #13 sleeps with rocks.

My Beautiful

FOR MABEL RAMSBURG WILT

Grandma Mabel, a laundry lady from Shepherdstown, West
Virginia, presses the letter to her lap, sighs Viceroys on the
south edge of her spongy double. Listens to *The Lone Ranger*,
looking out the non-existent window into Corona, into Queens,
into New York, into the West Caribbean, into Aruba, where the
beau who proposed is engineering oil for Flying A. Coaxes,
with grunts and shrugs, my pink Vick's Vapor Rub fingers from
the saw-toothed rim along her spine into the scar's crevasse.
Wherein waits the snake that ate her lung.

At 64

FOR DENISE

I wish I were the green hummingbird
helicoptering beside the fluted flowers
of the fire bush, the ochre snail
toting its cornucopia, the black indigo
holding the lion pose in the Catalonian
Jasmine, the Deepdigger scarab beetle
scraping the cemetery stones,
the unmined Andamookan opal
sat upon by the all-weather aborigine
whose swarthy hide is maintenance-free,
whose rutted skull sprouts ostrich-feathers.

Vermeer's Woman Weighing Gold

FOR DENISE

The Woman Weighing Gold is what she weighs. The balance
suspended from her thumb and forefinger is just a prop. The
tiger's eyes around her neck, merchant's coins, the twisted
yellow ribbon on the table are lead compared to her. The sun
has risen from within this pear-shaped Mary. Risen from the
well wherein she breathes. Risen through her pores to kindle
the cold walls. Risen to draw the curtains and open the window.
Risen so all things, Earth and sky, can spy the unimmaculate
birth.

In the Beginning
FOR DENISE

on the first day she gave birth
    after twelve hours of labor.
on the second day she nursed
    from the left and right breast.
on the third day she made pancakes
    and ham for her husband.
on the fourth day she sewed patches
    on the knees of his overalls.
on the fifth day she walked a mile
    to the river for fresh fish.
on the sixth day she milked the cow
    and watered the beans.
on the seventh day she listened
    to them suckle and snore.

Mark and I Were Not Supposed
MITCHELL AFB, 1956

Mark and I were not supposed

to play hardball in the field behind the shoemaker or in our good
clothes or the street or parking lots or the dark barn with witches
and coffins on the old polo field;

to go in the houses of strangers, or into the barracks or the NCO
Club, or off the base, to the dump, or on the flight line or railroad
tracks or the parade grounds, or near any planes, hangars, or
military offices;

to climb the rickety ladder to the tree house big boys built or
barbed wire fences or trees higher than our two-story brick house
or the coal pile or to the top of the tall swings, or onto the pyramid
of canvas-covered crates or the roof of the abandoned Sinclair
station;

to get separated, try to fly, build fires, beat up anybody or get
beaten up, snitch on each other, or pick flimsy switches when
we were getting whipped.

He Dug

His hands dug the sand of Moonlight Bay.
A Gulf Stream gale rattled the bananas.
A mile above his Air Force dad piloted the KC-135 to refuel
the F-104 enroute to Thule, Greenland.
He dug.
His mother delivered the weather on the island's only TV
station, in Hamilton.
He dug with his Scout knife.
His little league team hit grounders and flies across the harbor
on the diamond.
He dug.
The Ocean Monarch tied up at Saint George at the dock where
he'd learned to jig for jacks.
He dug with a cedar stick.
A flock of snowy egrets alighted on the mangroves.
Bermudian schoolboys in short pants and jackets shouted from
the football pitch across the street.
He dug.
The 5 p.m. horn sounded on base; Morris Minors queued up at
the main gate.
He dug with his belt buckle.
The men from the bait shop, Gombey dancers, sang as
they passed the banana patch.
He dug.
Barracuda chased a school of mullet into the wreck inside
Moonlight Bay.
He dug with a bloody conch shell.
Mom called him to dinner from the kitchen: Friday night pizza
and half a coke.

The poisonous toads that ate the centipedes hopped out of their limestone dens.

He dug.

Mom called again; the pizza was cold, and Dad was on his way.

High tide lapped the edge of the hole.

He dug.

Hammerheads surrounded a pilot who had ejected 12 miles out, near Kitchen's buoy.

He dug.

Canis Major passed. Taurus passed. Cancer passed. Leo passed. Ursa Major passed. Scorpio passed. Aquila passed. Aries passed.

He dug.

With tooth. Paw. Hoof. Horn. And claw.

Stuck With Snack Duty
CAMP LENAPE, 1963

Midnight. Stuck with late-snack duty. The paying scouts
surrounding the fire pit out back—mostly Tenderfeet and
Second-Class—char marshmallows, listen to Vic, helpful-
friendly-courteous-kind Life scout, re-cast the Jersey Devil tale
I told the breakfast crew at 6. I tune to the crickets' strings
instead: Paganini bowing an insanely-high vibrato. I push the
last tray of crusty, khaki-colored plastic cups into the spitting,
industrial Niagara. I heft the chocolate-scalded cauldron, the
one that carried oatmeal and pork and beans. Twice too big to
fit in, the army-issue pot lists like a ship in the mouth of the sink.
I open the hot water that runs cold. Through the gash in the
screen door, a thumb-sized horsefly comes buzzing. Neon green.
In an air-show arabesque, the emissary from the deep pine unties
my ankles. And exits the way it came.

Sitting in Ivy
QUEBEC, 1988

Whimpering and mystery persist on the other side of the rain.
Until the full moon's follow spot illuminates a critter.
Scurrying and scratching in the dirt between a tree and a mound.
In familiar ways. Like a cub. Like a kit. Skittish.

I'm outside the pup tent, unable to sleep. Legs webbed in wet
bushes, propped against a birch tree. In Army leftovers: beret
poncho, fatigue pants, and paratrooper boots soaked and cold.

The mound's a rubbish heap. I make out a truck spring, a
cushion, a fender, a tire, a mattress, a cracked bat. It stands up
on its hind legs and scans. It's a girl. Eight to ten-years old.
Shaggy-maned. Scaled in dirt. Half-clad in rags.

Lightning strikes nearby. My skull tolls. My spine and the birch
fuse. Our daughter, snug in the mummy bag with her mother,
mumbles. The skinny girl sniffs, hops like a wombat, pulls out
a paper bag. With her teeth.

Then she leaps in her hole—under the heap. I sit widest-eyed,
shivering, peering through the misty curtain—till sun outlines
a scorched pine, a boulder, sawed-off stumps. The itching
begins on the way home.

IRELAND

Queen Maeve

Three thousand years since the poet
strummed his seven-stringed lyre, peat
consecrates the timber and stone
of this northwestern home.
On this island stripped of sovereigns,
Maeve is every bit a queen.

All in black, by the hearth she sits.
And it is Jameson's whiskey she sips
rather than Dionysian wine.
And when we ask Maeve to sing,
she sings in Irish not Thracian,
an air more blessed than a hymn.

Surely muses bore the bard's spores
from the Hebrus to Eire's shore.

The Buses of Feda O'Donnail

The buses of Feda O'Donnail
stop to and from Dun na ngall
near the Letterkenny roundabout.
Two girls, 13 or 14 at most,
sit on the huge charcoal stone
by the stop, eating ice cream cones.
Their chin-length raspberry hair
leaps on their cheeks as they stare
at the profiles of people
framed by impatient vehicles.
Though they're coming of age
without rituals, without sages,
the two freckled faces have found
Earth's axis, center ground.

Apparition on Abbey Street

From a distance the man
on Abbey Street looks alive.
Yet when you arrive
you see he's an apparition
of a son-father-husband:
pothole eyes, petrol-soaked
polyesters, road-map raincoat,
rusted-out jowls, oil-slicked mane.
The once-respected phantom
strayed a step too far
from the Foggy Dew's door,
beyond the reach of neon.

Swallowed by the undertow,
he's now flotsam of its flow.

Poets' House

FOR BILLY COLLINS

Above us, Muckish takes the first puff,
Sucking Falcarrah's August sun up
To bake Charley's wirey black back
And my bushy green wool socks.

From the room of last night's communion
The smells of peat and John Powers come
On the jazz vibes of Wardell Gray
Fueling Michelle and Billy's play.

While the wordsmiths forge abs of steel
I try to conceal steaming oatmeal
With English soymilk but make a mess
On the oblong oak table. Did I miss?

It's funny. I don't feel hung over.
A regiment of raucous crows scours
Yesterday's mowed field for a scrap
Of last night's Irish bread. Charlie's nap

Is over. He bounds to the window
In time to see the out-of-key crows
Flee the hooves of recently fleeced sheep
Galloping from nothing I can see.

Billy and Michelle hold the crucifix
Position with two four-foot long sticks.
From my cracked bowl soymilk still drips

Onto the tile floor to Charlie's lips.

Muckish finishes its molten fag.
I sop the leakage with the white dishrag.
I hear Janice kid Michelle and Billy
Before she greets me, then brews coffee.

James gets back from town with *The Times*.
For us all, Janice reads the headline:
"President Clinton confesses sex!"
Charlie licks his whiskers, unimpressed.

Orpheus in Ballaghderg

Charlie McSwain was anchored
at the pit of the hill, outside the Shamrock's door.
A fire-faced, snow-haired scarecrow,

he hung over Kilmacrennam Road,
flagging his featherless limbs at motorists
driving to Ellistrin to give him a lift up the hill.

John McGinty, driving from Dublin
to Donegal, braked his Volvo coach up the rise
then let it glide all the way down. Charlie stepped in,

looked around, thanked John again
and again and again, then introduced himself. John
and his partner, Anne Marie, who had been speaking Irish,

switched to English to coax Charlie
up the steps. "Step in Charlie. So where is it
you want to be let off?" "The crossroads at the hilltop,"

Charlie said, standing beside John.
"My Maura's been taken. Dead. I don't think
I can go on living without her. Do you think I'll find

my Maura?" he asked Anne through
unguent eyes. "Is this the place, Charlie?"
John asked. "Right by the light, lad," said Charlie.

Charlie started to alight but
like a frightened parachute, wedged in
the portal, thanking the two over and over again.

The couple blessed Charlie McSwain,
prayed that he would leave and let them go.
John said, "Watch your step getting out, Charlie."

Finally, Anne stepped down, gripped
his black sleeve, and ushered him out. Charlie
took two baby steps toward home. The Volvo coach

ferried its passenger toward Falcarrah.
In his rearview mirror, John saw Charlie turned
around by the tide, carried down by the undertow.

In Clonbara

FOR DAVID CRAIG

The sky is still light at ten
when at home we would wend
our way to our rooms to weave
a carpet of our day's deeds.

In Clonbarra we clamor
for song, verse, and story,
so we leave the meeting hall
with its peat hearth and wide walls

and go to the kitchen table
where we'd earlier assembled
to share salmon, ratatouille,
and Australian Chablis.

It is the hour for John Power.
It is the hour to honor
the tenant farmers and crofters,
to toast bards and troubadours.

David sings a Highland ballad.
Jimmy starts "Arthur Macbride"
on guitar and Janice joins in.
Maeve intones "Amhran Na Bhfiann."

For four days Muckish Mountain
has been covered by a curtain
extending from the ocean
inland to Kilmacrenan.

Now in the Dun na ngall dusk
as we six sing "Carrickfergus,"
its trapezoidal shadow
appears through the kitchen window.

By the time the jig is done
the boar's brawny back is gone;
the window which throws back our joy
is a lustrous slab of coal.

AROUND SAN ANN

The Lime Green Tree Frog

hides behind the window's white
siding until sundown squawks
and watches

greybeard in the blue room
toss and turn on thorns

the magenta four-o'clocks
rope intoxicated moon moths
greybeard mistakes for hummingbirds

the one-legged vet
park his camouflage Econoline
by the square's garden of memories
and wash under the faucet

the black and blue girl
crawl from under Saint Anthony
School, find half an ant sandwich
in the trash, and chew it while she swings

the Burmese Python lumber from
the culvert beside city hall to bait
wild hogs with acorns at the base
of the square's pyramidal oaks

Andromeda rise from the cemetery
in the west on the back of Pegasus
and bed down behind the monastery
with the Orionids

greybeard's best feature, sleep
without dreams, sieve through
the screen and feed the ancestors.

Missus Slug's Dried Slime

FOR JOHN LILY

Missus slug, was that a cellophane noodle you drug back
and forth last night across the sidewalk from the rose bush
outside my bedroom to the road? And the night before—
were you unfolding your version of the flat hose
the firepeople next door fold and unfold?
And the night before that—were you slobbering drunk
on the dregs of Pancho's sangria I spilled on the Amaryllis?
Or figure skating, skywriting, dervish-dancing, transcribing
the music of the spheres for those with ears to hear?
Or maybe, like John Lilly's dolphin friend, you're back.
Again and again. Patiently persevering. Offering metaphor
after metaphor. For slow mind.

Moth

FOR DAVE OLIPHANT

When I shower in the morning
I watch you performing some austerity
flat against the tile on your knees,
kissing the mildew,
your slim fingers wedged
above your hood,
your brown flecked habit
swept back like an arrowhead.

Are you rapt in Benedict's divinizing
light, your brain waves beating delta
like a hibernating bear
while the godmind soars?
Do you sleep
face down in the filthy street
cloaked in holy bedspreads?

These days monks are dividing
and mendicants are multiplying.
What does it mean?
In the Dark Ages
monasticism and dereliction
ran hand and hand.

As I step in,
I nudge you with the soap;
you flutter up drunkenly
into the folds of the faded garden
and are forgotten
by the time I rinse.

But when I pull away the veil
and step out to dry
you crawl out from the crease
where you've been contemplating.
Half in jest
I prod you with my towel,
just to test your piety.
Like a sot
you lumber up the polyester
and needle through an eyelet
to the other side.

The Malachite Mole

who lives in the Zuni clay
jar in the foyer told me to meet him out
back at midnight by the badger
-sized hole dug under the hibiscus, into which
I'd been throwing compost. I drank strong
tea, PG Tips, to stay awake and met him at the hole
(of which I'd been afraid) in my scuffed paratrooper
boots and overalls (which he told me to remove). He was
bigger in person, the size of my human hand, the same size
I became after I did what he did: nudged aside the scraps of
last night's cabbage with my nose (which telescoped like
Pinocchio's). We spoke by clacking our typewriter-key teeth.
(I punctured my tongue.) And by thumping, scratching, and
slapping our forepaws the size of centerfielder's mitts against
the clay, stone, and roots that lined the deepening hole, enroute
to what he said was a particularly rich bed of earthworms thirty
feet beneath the Bodhisattva in my bedroom. I wondered how
I was breathing. He told me my mole lungs were reusing
oxygen I had inhaled at the surface. I was happy that I'd been
shutting my eyes when I walked the nighttime streets of San
Antonio. Happy that I'd dug a new drain field all alone. Happy
that I'd stopped the pest control man from spraying under the
house.

4 O'clocks

purse their coral
lips, pucker up, poke out
their braided tongues,
play dead when
the sun comes
over zephyr hills.

but when the sun prostrates
behind san ann cemetery
cedars, they yawn
on their chartreuse
skeletal stalks,

yawn till each
blossom opens its five
balinese fans, till each
six-barreled pistol
blasts its manichewitz,
guzzled by sparrow-sized
moon moths.

Ordinary Alchemy
FOR YASMINE

When aluminum and copper get it right. Like when the red king
and white queen wed. Like the lodge, in the South, when sweat
enters sweet grass. When water's poured on the stone people,
imploring the Powers to ease some suffering, all suffering,
and the stone people's hiss becomes the symphony in your head,
on which you're pouring water. And you can't help but slump,
and the steam, once it kisses the bamboo and canvas cap, blossoms
back in four directions. Embalming your submarining shoulders
in sparks. Of snow. Then, in the sodden hay of space, inches
below your dripping nose tip, you see it, them, through swabbed
eyes: planets panting like panthers, never detected by your or
anyone else's telescope.

The Black Bear

male was "harvested by Natives
in British Columbia," the Ute said.
I stroked and stroked his boneless back
before hiding him in my rolled sleeping bag.
At home the bear stretched under my skin
on the Tibetan carpet or scrolled under
my neck. When Yasmine came home,
he crossed my heart.

That night we sweated in the backyard.
I sat where the rock people singed my knees,
with my bent back to the black West
and sang Paiute bear songs shaman
Ray Stone had saved for his father who
had saved them for his father who
had known the Sierra Nevada bear people
would become cartoons.

In dream time, our old man returned
young and jovial, more buff than ever.
Clad in form-fitting black, glowing
like lodge stones, he stood in our backyard
that he had tractored flat.
After staring to get my attention,
he waved his glossy onyx driver
like a war club

and scanned the North horizon—
without pecans or oaks or palms,
without sweat lodge or shed, or fire pit,
without fences or neighbors or orange groves.
Then pressed a white tee and ball
into the green stubble, bent over,
rooted his spread legs, waggled his hips,
and showed me how it was done.

We Told the Animals

    they could stay in our backyard
where we dig kivas among the blackberries,
where elephant ears are taller than elephants,
where emerald hummingbirds siphon four-o'clocks for 24 hours,
where we start stout fires that neighbors never see, to heat rocks
    from Carolina for a sweat lodge under one of three pecan trees,
where a black three-legged rabbit raises abandoned kittens,
where six-inch snails leave cellophane trails up and down silver
    oaks that stretch from middle earth to the highest rung of heaven,
where the spiked tentacles of roses who were here before the
    house have long-since subsumed the post and wire fence,
where one naps on a hammock and wakes a week later.

We called in the turkeys from the East where the golf course
    is expanding its sewage treatment plant.
We called in the boar tribe from the South where their swamp
    will become the newest wing of San Antonio Self-Storage.
We called in the bobcats and deer from the West, across Palm
    Avenue, where a forest was razed and a cemetery will be born
    in its place.
We called in the possums, raccoons, and skunks from the grapefruit
    groves to the North, which will one day, when the recession ends,
    become San Ann's fourth convenience store.
We called down the red-shouldered hawks from Above, whose
    parapets were razed for the bigger and better fire station.
And we called up the worms, the gators, the moccasins, and the
    skinks from Below where the last drops of Lake Louise were
    sucked to flush the toilets of Saint Pete.

San Antonio Boars

When the *Saint Pete Times* delivery truck stuck it in third,
they were truffling in the muck east of the storage facility.
Mom and Dad, up to their steel drums, kids up to their latex
snouts. By the time sun slithered down the bricks of Saint
Anthony School and the first first grader had been disgorged,
the brood were bunked in the bowels of the as yet unpaved
Cannon Ranch. But with midnight's maraschino moon, they
were frisky. Mom and Dad jumpstarted the Beer Garden's
fountain wherein their mottled octet bubble-bathed the day's
stain.

The Great Depression

Blue Wendy, a mid-wife under San Ann's first physician, hung out in Red Door cottage, whose cube core was his operating room. The third and fourth arms of Avalokitesvara, she delivered newborns as well as tumors, both first and last breaths. Until her heart broke over the miscarriage she buried in the backyard under wild roses that no longer bloom but bite better than barbed wire.

Though buried in the sand of San Ann Cemetery, Wendy preferred to wade through her lake of tears--in our day waiting in our living room that was his waiting room and at our night pacing between our kitchen that was his porch and the wild rose that barricades the back yard.

For sixty of our years she battered the card houses of then and now, of love and loss, of cube and cottage, of rose and thorn, of solids and specters. Until one pre-dawn, when a thunder storm performed Beethoven's Ninth on Red Door's tin roof. And we saw the shade of Wendy, surf stiffly through a ghostly railroad train of rooms, that telescoped cross Curley and the cemetery into a glowing keyhole in the western clouds.

Saint Leo Waterworks

Once one could peer through the iron grate into the maw of
the waterworks; once one could even, if the rusted lock had
been left open and the moon was new, grow down the iron
ladder into the cool gloom and feel one's way amid the maze
of monster roots and lead intestines till the cat eyes came.
But now Security has replaced the grate with a light-tight steel
box, a turret affair, fastened with four stainless steel locks.
And the closest one can come now to the minotaur who lives
under the monastery is to sit atop the shiny mahogany steel
box and hear its baritone groans.

In the Afterlife

black boars the size of musk oxen
still eat acorns in San Antonio Park;
the interloping cock with bronze secondaries
who crowed day and night from the oak limb
still has his beak, comb, blade, and wattles
but doesn't bloody his harem of hens;
the eight-foot indigo snake
that recyclers bisected with a shovel
still sheds its fish-net stocking
on our front-door welcome mat;
a skinny Rip Van Winkle,
wearing a straw hat, scuffed black boots,
and the coveralls in which he slept,
looks like the trunk of a cedar
that once distracted foul shooters;
on his shoulders, which are also limbs,
sit the screech owl, crow, and ruby-throated
hummingbird who speak for him;
a few feet from his roots the three year- old him
who stayed on the Azores, the ten year-old him
who stayed on Long Island, and the thirteen year-old him
who stayed on Bermuda, play mumbly peg, looking
like brothers.

Weeki Wachee Mermaids

In winter, we put in downstream of the source where the tour
boats turn back. Led by meteors of mullet, our orange kayak
unzips the river from morning to mid-day. From east to west.
From mud hens to manatee. From shallow, wide shoulders of
eel grass to steep waists of cypress, oak, and palm. When the
river deepens and bends northward, we tie up and dive from the
lap of a Medusa-like cypress crossed with boards. Cool rain
falls like confetti. We shiver. That's when I hear their siren,
the two-toned antiquated drone of their john boats. Like an otter,
I tread water, stare into a fairy tale.
The men, looking Norman Rockwell, carefully steer short of me.
Nod, rope their scratched khaki out-board to a horizontal scrub
palm. Speak in jolly viola tones. In what I guess to be a dialect
of French. Like a painting of Delvaux, they--grandmother,
mother, daughter—stand silent sails in the center of the second
boat. Even after their men rope them to the palm. The women
hide their fins in cardigans. Their Olympian grins. Their
sons, clad in permanent-press cutoffs, clamor up their fathers'
backs to reach the diving tree's first rung. But there the sons
stop. Cock their heads backwards and down. Won't climb the
crosses to the crow's nest till their mermaid mothers' sign.

The Vacant Birdfeeder

FOR DENISE

Longing for your song
I built a birdfeeder

of cedar shaped like
a Shinto temple.

Wrens and sparrows gathered
on its open porches.

Waxwings alighted in
the nearby Virginia pine.

From the living room
I heard them chirp at dawn.

I crept to the kitchen
to part the lacy curtains

careful not to scare them
because they seemed to hear.

When the weather turned cold
and the day contracted,

mockingbirds screeched
from the pine's high boughs.

Shaggy stray cats
prowled through the choleas,

their bodies stretched like bows,
eyes arrowed five feet up.

The cats were nightmares
shrieking near my window,

peeing on the front porch,
breeding in the driveway

before their dawn stakeout
of the vacant birdfeeder.

A Red Arabian

A red Arabian breathed on
my window last night.
It was so dark I couldn't see
my hand, but I knew
the horse was the rust
of my youthful beard.
He snorted. Stomped the ground.
Called me out.
When I got there his hooves
panned the horizon.
Gradually his lasso closed
around the house.
The rusty whirlwind stirred the earth
where the horse had been.
Feeling faint from the fury,
I gulped thunder.
The red Arabian stood there
nostrils to my nose.
Filling me like a pillar.

Lost on the Longestdarkestday

without a tag
on whatwasonce a trail
from the front
to the back
through elephantear tapestries
crepemyrtle tentacles
tangerinetree morningstars
that doubledare the saw
fleshcutting shrubs whomilove
but don'tknow by name
under the massivesaggingfourarms
of the oak thatsomedays
is Atlas somedays Poseidon
somedays Yggrasil somedays
a Druid, somedays the sundance
pole somedays myspine
somedays mybrothereric
inandout of holesdug by moles
andvoles andpossum
andmice andsnakes
andraccons andarmadillos
andbobcats andcatsanddogs
intothehole
idugunder the pecantree
fromwhichfourdaysfromnow
imightholyhopingcrawl

RAVEN

Raven Contemplates Cochima
('LITTLE BEAR' IN APACHE)

Twenty-seven's engine,
thundering onto Main,
tumbles Raven from red
reverie into the bed
of Cochima's persimmon
pickup. "Why's the godson
of Geronimo hanging
out in San Ann, spraying
medicine water? Could
the old shaman who died
with his power have come
back to Disney prison?
Look at those sandhill cranes
strutting like they own Main;
if I did that, they'd run
me over." The two iron-
headed pharaohs traverse
Penn., arresting Hummers,
to spring the anesthetized
flock of flamingos skewered
to the grass rectangle
in front of city hall.

Raven Craves Infatuation

From the roof of San Ann Market,
Raven swoops at something cute.
"That dragonfly's upside-down in
the fountain," exclaims Heineken.
"It's a Rufous Hummingbird," "What's
it doing on the Southeast Coast"?
asks Malbec, who snaps a photo
with his phone. "Damn bird doesn't show
up." "Look, now it's showering
like a person. If it can sing,
I'll cage it." Bored, Raven squawks
his fast fans into chicken hawks.
Then he, in his pugnacious shape,
pirates ham quiche from their plates.

Raven as Tiger Swallowtail

Raven, waving his wand
in the manner he's seen
Ethiopian queens
coat their toes, tints his frond
tips orange and turquoise,
then flutters from the rail
like fall to the Royal
Palm by the firehouse
on Pennsylvania Ave.
Landing in the jasmine
that skirts its trunk, Raven
surfs the Star-of David waves.

Raven as Town Crier

On the water
tower, town crier,
Raven, declares:

"Three opossum
run over on
Pompanic. Seven

rabbits with slit
throats in their hutch
hid in red lips.

A sack of frogs
gigged in the bog
north of Palm Ridge.

Armadillos
shot with arrows
for digging holes

in Laurel Court.
The recycling truck
butted a young buck

on Hartman Road.
Hoards of star-nosed
moles exterminated

from the homeless
development west
of Palm. A nest

of gopher turtles
poisoned by oil
dumped in the jungle

behind the greasy
spoon. A family
of migratory

sandhills cranes hit
by a hearse in flight
from a gravesite.

Raven as Prayer Wheel

Raven delights being
a lair where six winds spin,
where the dreaded sphinxes
of the six directions
dance. And for these weeks
their breaths employ his beak
the tower where he spiels
is an iron prayer wheel.

Raven Outside City Hall

To woo the city clerk, Raven
plays his debonair crooner cousin,
red-winged black, and has his back
cracked by the chiro, so he can snap
his secondaries and primaries
while he warbles "O-ka-lee, O-ka-lee,
Look-at-me" from the magnolia near
by. From the dusk, Venus, his former
flame, hears his shtick and flim-flams
his carpe diem. When his new flame
comes out, she burns for the basil-
lemony perfume of the magnolia,
but seethes at the rough-hewn "Cr-ruck,
Cr-ruck, Cr-ruck, Cr-cruck" of the huckster.

Raven Spies Panther

Once a turquoise nugget
in a necklace that stretched
to the Gulf, the lake fled.
Its nest is occupied

by scrub willow and packs
of wild plastic bags. Raven,
borrowing the goggles
of burrowing owl,

sees the eyes of panther
needling the beryl air
once wended by gators,
carp, bass, turtles, otters.

Chrome claws creep up the bank
beside the oil tank.
Behind the ancient jail,
they paw the earth and wail.

Raven on the Equinox

No rain for three weeks,
and nights no longer freeze.
Raven crunches cat's food
after chasing Cane Toad
from the bowl. He hears singing
out back. "Why's gray beard fussing
with the kiva? It's too dry
for a fire." So he flies
to the kiva's bamboo door.
Inside, the trolling geezer
lies on his back, East to West,
and buries his bony chest,
ribs, abdomen, and groin
under cantloupe-sized stones.
Raven fire sticks old man's
corn-cob pipe so he can
puff prayers to Up, Down,
Inside, and All-Around.

Raven and the Glowing Stones

Though cold, the lodge stones
glow, casting a column

down through the aquifer,
up through the conifer.

Raven dons his polyester
kite suit with scimitar

wings and Cadillac fins
and joins sulphurs, humming-

birds, and dragonflies
who effortlessly ride

the copper cylinder's
circumambulating winds.

Raven and Vast Self

FOR JOSEPH RAEL

Raven removes his overcoat,
exhales like a centrifuge,
emptying himself of air,
water, fire, and earth,
painting the Up and Down
and the four horizons.

By letting breath's
leash loose, by turning
the cup inside-out,
by becoming a black
hole, Vast Self grows.

When breath reels back
from the boundaries,
when wild beds down
in the stable, Raven's
temporary eddy resumes.
Never the same.

www.ingramcontent.com/pod-product-compliance
Lightning Source LLC
Chambersburg PA
CBHW072358090426
42741CB00012B/3075